Our Favorite

Cheap & Easy recipes

Copyright 2007, Gooseberry Patch
Third Printing, March, 2010

Flatten chicken between wax paper using a rolling pin and
a little muscle... just toss the paper and there's no mess!

2

Crispy Taco Chicken

Makes 4 servings

3/4 c. dry bread crumbs
1-1/4 oz. pkg. taco seasoning
   mix

4 boneless, skinless chicken
   breasts
1/2 c. mayonnaise

Combine bread crumbs and taco seasoning; set aside. Spread chicken with mayonnaise; coat with bread crumb mixture. Arrange on an aluminum foil-lined baking sheet; bake at 425 degrees for 20 minutes, or until juices run clear when chicken is pierced with a fork.

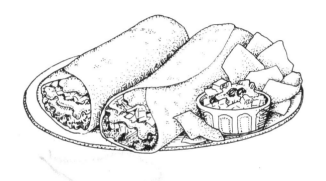

To spice up familiar casserole recipes, use various cheeses
like smoked hot pepper or Pepper Jack. Cayenne pepper,
chopped pickled jalapeños or fresh jalapeño peppers
will also turn up the heat!

Quick-as-Lightning Enchiladas   *Makes 4 servings*

16-oz. jar chunky salsa
3/4 c. mayonnaise
4 c. cooked chicken, diced

8 to 10   8-inch flour tortillas
16-oz. pkg. shredded Colby-
    Jack cheese, divided

Mix together salsa and mayonnaise; stir in chicken. Spoon about
1/2 cup chicken mixture down the center of each tortilla; sprinkle
each with 1/4 cup cheese and roll up. Place tortillas seam-side down
in a greased 13"x9" baking pan. Spoon remaining chicken mixture
evenly over top of tortillas. Sprinkle with remaining cheese. Bake at
350 degrees for 15 minutes, or until cheese is melted.

Set a regular theme for each night of the week...Italian Night,
Soup & Salad Night, Mexican Night or Casserole Night, based
on your family's favorites. Meal planning is a snap!

Instant Chicken Parmesan

Makes 4 to 6 servings

28-oz. jar spaghetti sauce
4 to 6 frozen breaded chicken
    patties
4 to 6 slices provolone cheese

1 to 2 T. grated Parmesan
    cheese
Optional: cooked thin spaghetti

Spread sauce in an ungreased 13"x9" baking pan; arrange frozen chicken patties on top. Place a slice of provolone on top of each patty; sprinkle with Parmesan cheese. Bake, covered, at 350 degrees for 20 minutes. Uncover and bake for an additional 5 to 10 minutes, or until cheese is bubbly. Serve over cooked spaghetti, if desired.

If a recipe calls for stewed tomatoes, take advantage
of Mexican or Italian-style. They already have the
seasonings added, so there are fewer ingredients
for you to buy and measure!

Sweet & Tangy Pork

Makes 4 servings

1 T. oil
4 boneless pork steaks
10-3/4 oz. can tomato soup
2 T. vinegar
1 T. Worcestershire sauce

1 T. brown sugar, packed
8-oz. can pineapple tidbits,
   drained and 1/4 c. juice
   reserved

Heat oil in a skillet over medium heat. Add steaks and cook until golden on both sides; drain. Stir in soup, vinegar, sauce, brown sugar, pineapple and reserved juice. Cover and simmer over low heat for 5 to 10 minutes, until pork is cooked through.

It's a snap to slice uncooked meat...
pop it in the freezer for 10 to 15 minutes first.

Orange-Pork Stir-Fry

Makes 4 servings

1-oz. pkg. Italian salad dressing
   mix
1/4 c. orange juice
1/4 c. oil
2 T. soy sauce

1 lb. pork loin, cut into strips
16-oz. pkg. frozen Oriental
   vegetable blend, thawed
2-1/2 c. cooked rice

Mix together dressing mix, juice, oil and soy sauce. Combine one tablespoon of dressing mixture and pork strips in a large skillet over medium heat. Cook and stir for 4 to 5 minutes, or until meat is no longer pink. Add vegetables and remaining dressing mixture; cook and stir until vegetables are crisp-tender. Serve over cooked rice.

A smiling face is half the meal.

-Latvian Proverb

Oodles of Noodles Chili Bake

Makes 4 servings

1 lb. ground beef, browned
  and drained
15-oz. can chili
1 c. shredded Cheddar cheese,
  divided

14-1/2 oz. can diced tomatoes
15-oz. can corn, drained
12-oz. pkg. egg noodles,
  cooked

Mix beef, chili, 3/4 cup cheese, tomatoes, corn and noodles together
in a lightly greased 13"x9" baking pan; sprinkle with remaining
cheese. Bake at 350 degrees until heated through, about 20 minutes.

Keep browned ground beef on hand for easy meal prep.
Crumble several pounds of beef onto a baking pan and
bake at 350 degrees until browned through, stirring
often. Drain well and pack recipe portions in freezer bags.

Quick Pizza Casserole

Makes 6 servings

1 lb. ground beef, browned
    and drained
14-oz. jar pizza sauce
8-oz. pkg. shredded
    mozzarella cheese

3/4 c. biscuit baking mix
1-1/2 c. milk
2 eggs

Place beef in an ungreased 8"x8" baking pan; top with pizza sauce and cheese. Combine baking mix, milk and eggs in a mixing bowl; stir well until smooth. Pour over cheese; bake at 400 degrees for 30 to 35 minutes, until golden on top.

Mmm...mashed potatoes are the ultimate comfort food.
Simmer potatoes in chicken broth instead
of water for delicious flavor.

Smothered Chicken

Makes 4 servings

1 T. oil
1/4 c. onion, finely chopped
1/4 c. green pepper, finely
   chopped
1/4 c. celery, finely chopped

1 lb. boneless, skinless chicken
   breasts or thighs
3/4-oz. pkg. mushroom gravy
   mix
12-oz. can evaporated milk

Heat oil in a skillet. Sauté vegetables over medium-high heat
for 2 minutes, or until crisp-tender. Add chicken; cook for 6 to
7 minutes per side until golden. Blend together gravy mix and milk;
stir into skillet. Bring to a boil; reduce heat, cover and simmer for
15 minutes, until chicken juices run clear. To serve, spoon gravy
from pan over chicken.

Try a new topping on casserole dishes...sprinkle on shredded cheese, fresh bread crumbs or crushed chow mein noodles. And to keep the topping crisp, don't cover the casserole dish during baking.

Chicken & Stuffing Bake

Makes 6 servings

1/2 c. water
1 T. margarine
4 c. herb-flavored stuffing mix
6 boneless, skinless chicken
    breasts, halved

1/8 t. paprika
10-3/4 oz. can cream of
    mushroom soup
1/3 c. milk
1 t. dried parsley

Bring water and margarine to a boil in a large saucepan; remove from heat. Stir in stuffing mix. Spoon mixture across center of a lightly greased 3-quart casserole dish. Arrange chicken on each side of stuffing. Sprinkle with paprika; set aside. Combine soup, milk and parsley; pour over chicken. Bake, covered, at 350 degrees for 15 minutes. Uncover; bake for an additional 15 minutes, or until chicken is cooked through.

There's no need to be formal with one-pot meals...
set the pot in the center of the dinner table
and let everyone help themselves!

Italian Bean & Sausage Pasta *Makes 4 servings*

6-oz. pkg. smoked turkey
  sausage, halved and sliced
14-1/2 oz. can Italian stewed
  tomatoes
14-1/2 oz. can Italian green
  beans, drained
2 c. cooked rotini pasta
1/4 c. grated Parmesan cheese

Cook sausage in a skillet over medium heat until browned. Add
tomatoes and beans; bring to a boil for 2 to 3 minutes. Stir in pasta
and heat through; sprinkle with cheese.

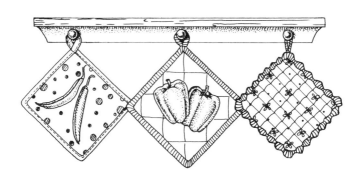

A speedy side...sauté frozen green beans until crisp-tender and toss with a jar of roasted red peppers.

Tender Pork Chops & Rice   *Makes 4 to 6 servings*

4 to 6 pork chops
1 T. oil
10-3/4 oz. can cream of
   mushroom soup

4-oz. can sliced mushrooms,
   drained and liquid reserved
2 c. long-cooking rice,
   uncooked

Brown pork chops lightly in oil in a skillet; drain and set aside.
Combine soup, reserved liquid from mushrooms and enough water to
equal 3 cups; mix well and pour into skillet. Stir in mushrooms and
rice; top with pork chops. Cover and simmer for 30 to 45 minutes,
or until rice is tender.

Make this lasagna the night before and store in the
fridge for an even speedier dinner. Just add
10 minutes to the cooking time...so easy!

Easy Cheesy Lasagna

Makes 4 to 6 servings

1/2 lb. ground beef
26-oz. jar spaghetti sauce
8-oz. pkg. wide egg noodles,
    cooked

8-oz. pkg. shredded
    mozzarella cheese
1 c. cottage cheese
1 c. grated Parmesan cheese

Brown ground beef in a saucepan; drain. Stir sauce into beef; simmer for 5 minutes. Add noodles, mozzarella cheese and cottage cheese; stir together and place in a greased 2-quart casserole dish. Sprinkle with Parmesan cheese; bake at 350 degrees for 30 minutes.

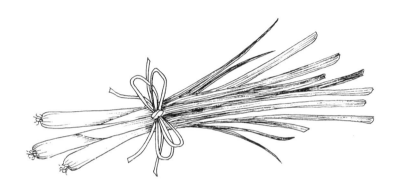

Frozen packages of chopped onion, cut-up green peppers,
and stir-fry vegetables can take minutes off mealtime
preparations...no chopping, mincing or dicing!
It's already done for you.

Swiss Steak Dinner

Makes 4 servings

1 T. olive oil
2 lbs. beef cube steaks
29-oz. can tomato sauce
14-3/4 oz. can beef gravy

28-oz. pkg. frozen diced
  potatoes with green pepper
  and onion, thawed

Heat olive oil in a skillet over medium heat; brown steaks. Drain; place in a large stockpot. Add tomato sauce, gravy and potatoes; bring to a boil. Reduce heat to medium; simmer for 10 minutes, or until potatoes are tender.

Hollow out round crusty loaves for bread bowls...
they make soup even tastier!

Quick & Easy Beef Stew

Makes 4 servings

1 T. oil
1 lb. boneless beef sirloin steak,
   cut into 1-inch cubes
10-3/4 oz. can French onion
   soup

10-3/4 oz. can tomato soup
1 T. Worcestershire sauce
24-oz. pkg. frozen stew
   vegetables

Heat oil in a large skillet over medium heat; add beef. Cook and stir until browned and juices have evaporated. Add soups, sauce and vegetables; bring to a boil. Reduce heat; cover and cook over low heat for 10 to 15 minutes, until vegetables are tender.

A simple crockery bowl filled to the brim with ripe pears, apples
and other fresh fruit makes an oh-so-simple centerpiece...
it's a great way to encourage healthy snacking too!

Simple Tuna One-Dish

Makes 7 to 9 servings

2 T. butter
1/2 c. onion, diced
2 T. all-purpose flour
1 c. milk
2 6-oz. cans tuna, drained

15-oz. can peas, drained
3/4 t. salt
1/4 t. pepper
8-oz. tube refrigerated biscuits

Melt butter over medium heat in a 1-1/2 quart heat-resistant baking dish. Sauté onion until tender. Add flour and milk; stir well over low heat until smooth and thickened. Add tuna, peas, salt and pepper; mix well. Top with biscuits; bake at 425 degrees for 15 minutes, or until biscuits are golden.

Pick up a bundle of fresh flowers when you shop for groceries.
Tucked into a pitcher or glass jar, even humble daisies
are charming and cheerful for a centerpiece.

Tuna Pasta Primavera

Makes 4 to 6 servings

8-oz. pkg. rotini pasta,
    uncooked
2 heads broccoli, cut into
    flowerets
4 carrots, peeled and chopped
12-oz. can tuna, drained

1/2 c. mayonnaise
1/4 c. milk
1/4 c. grated Parmesan cheese
1/2 t. garlic powder
1/2 t. dried basil
1/4 t. pepper

Cook pasta according to package directions, adding broccoli and carrots to cooking water during last 5 minutes of cooking. Drain and return to pan; keep warm. Mix remaining ingredients together and add to pasta; toss to coat.

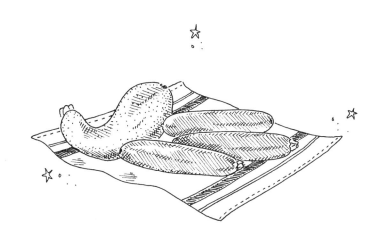

Zucchini and other summer squash make tasty main dishes and are easily swapped out in recipes. Try substituting yellow crookneck or pattypan for zucchini in any favorite recipe.

Zucchini & Sausage Casserole   *Makes 4 to 6 servings*

1 lb. ground pork sausage
1-1/2 c. instant rice, uncooked
2 c. zucchini, diced
1/2 c. onion, thinly sliced
16-oz. can stewed tomatoes

1 c. hot water
1 t. mustard
1 t. garlic salt
1/8 t. pepper
1 c. shredded Cheddar cheese

Brown sausage in a large skillet over medium heat. Drain, reserving 2 tablespoons drippings in skillet. Return sausage to skillet; add rice, zucchini and onion. Cook and stir until zucchini and onion are tender. Add remaining ingredients except cheese; bring to a boil. Cover; reduce heat and simmer for 5 minutes. Top with cheese; cover again until cheese is melted.

It's easy to freshen up yesterday's crusty rolls or
loaf of bread. Simply sprinkle with water and bake
at 400 degrees for 6 to 8 minutes.

Stir-Fry Vegetables

Makes 4 to 6 servings

3/4 c. pineapple juice
1 T. sugar
1 T. lemon juice
1-1/2 t. cornstarch
1 t. soy sauce
4 t. oil
1 c. broccoli flowerets

1 c. carrot, peeled and sliced
1 c. cauliflower flowerets
1 c. celery, sliced
1 c. red or green pepper, cut
   into bite-size pieces
1 c. sugar peas, stemmed

Combine first 5 ingredients in a bowl; mix well and set aside. Heat oil in a skillet; add broccoli, carrot, cauliflower and celery. Cook and stir for 2 minutes over medium-high heat. Add pepper and sugar peas; cook and stir an additional 2 minutes. Add pineapple juice mixture. Cover and bring to a boil; continue boiling for one minute.

Pick up some paper plates and cups in seasonal designs...
they'll make dinner fun when you're in a hurry
and clean-up will be a breeze.

Salmon Patties

Makes 5 to 6 servings

15-1/2 oz. can salmon,
   drained and flaked
1/2 c. round buttery crackers,
   crushed
1/2 T. dried parsley
1/2 t. lemon zest

1 T. lemon juice
2 green onions, sliced
1 egg, beaten
2 T. oil
5 to 6 English muffins, split
   and toasted

Combine first 7 ingredients; form into 5 to 6 patties. Heat oil in a skillet over medium heat. Cook patties 4 to 5 minutes on each side, until golden. Serve on English muffins topped with Cucumber Sauce.

Cucumber Sauce:

1/3 c. cucumber, chopped
1/4 c. plain yogurt

1/4 c. mayonnaise
1/4 t. dried tarragon

Combine all ingredients; chill until ready to serve.

Make a delicious honey-mustard dip for chicken nuggets
with 2/3 cup honey and 1/3 cup mustard. Try different
kinds of honey and mustard to create flavor variations.

Oven-Baked Chicken Fingers

Makes 6 servings

1 c. dry Italian bread crumbs
2 T. grated Parmesan cheese
1 clove garlic, minced

1/4 c. oil
6 boneless, skinless chicken
  breasts

Shake bread crumbs and cheese together in a plastic zipping bag; set aside. Combine garlic and oil in a small bowl; set aside. Flatten chicken to 1/2-inch thickness; cut into one-inch wide strips. Dip strips in oil mixture; coat with crumb mixture. Arrange on a greased baking sheet; bake at 350 degrees for 20 minutes, turning after 10 minutes.

Ripe red tomatoes and sweet onions from the farmers' market
are such a treat in summer! Serve them simply, with just
a dash of oil & vinegar and a sprinkle of fresh basil.

Lemon-Pepper Fish Dinner

Makes 4 servings

1 lb. frozen cod, thawed
16-oz. pkg. frozen stir-fry
   vegetables
salt to taste
1 t. lemon-pepper seasoning

1 t. dried rosemary
1 c. tomato juice
2-1/2 T. grated Parmesan
   cheese

Line a 13"x9" baking dish with aluminum foil. Place cod in dish and cover with vegetables. Sprinkle with salt, lemon-pepper seasoning and rosemary. Pour tomato juice over all; sprinkle with Parmesan cheese. Bake at 400 degrees for 20 to 25 minutes, or until fish flakes and vegetables are tender.

Cook a double batch of rice, then freeze half in a plastic freezer bag for another meal. When you're ready to use the frozen rice, just microwave on high for one minute per cup to thaw, 2 to 3 minutes per cup to warm it through. Fluff with a fork...ready to use!

Chinese Fried Rice

Makes 4 to 6 servings

3 T. oil
1 c. cooked chicken, pork or
    shrimp, chopped
2 eggs, beaten
3/4 t. salt

1/2 t. pepper
3 c. cooked rice, chilled
2 T. soy sauce
Garnish: 2 green onions,
    snipped

Heat oil in a deep skillet over medium heat. Add meat and cook for one minute. Add eggs, salt and pepper; cook, stirring constantly, until eggs are set. Add rice and soy sauce; cook, stirring constantly, for about 5 minutes, until rice is heated through. Garnish with green onions.

Save time on kitchen clean-up...always use a spatter
screen when frying in a skillet or Dutch oven.

Spicy Sausage & Rice

Makes 4 servings

1 lb. hot ground pork sausage	6.9-oz. pkg. chicken-flavored
1 onion, diced	rice vermicelli mix
Optional: 1 green pepper, diced	2-1/2 c. water

Cook sausage in a skillet over medium heat until it begins to brown; add onion and pepper, if using. Continue to cook until sausage is done and onion is tender; drain. Add seasoning packet from rice mix; stir well. Add rest of mix; sauté 3 to 4 minutes, stirring frequently. Add water and bring to a boil. Cover and reduce heat; simmer for 20 to 25 minutes, until rice is tender.

Keep a can of non-stick vegetable spray near
the stove...quickly spritz on a casserole
dish or skillet for easy clean-up later.

Salisbury Steak

Makes 4 to 6 servings

1 lb. ground beef
1/2 to 3/4 c. saltine crackers,
  crushed
1 egg, beaten
1/4 c. onion, chopped

1/2 t. salt
pepper to taste
1/2 c. water
10-1/2 oz. can brown gravy

Combine ground beef, cracker crumbs, egg, onion, salt and pepper
in a large mixing bowl. Form into 6 to 8 patties; set aside. Combine
water and gravy; pour into a large skillet over medium heat. Add
patties. Cover and simmer for 25 to 30 minutes, turning
halfway through.

Bouillon granules are quick-dissolving for use
in any recipe...keep a jar in your pantry!

Speedy Beef Stroganoff

1 lb. beef round steak
1/4 c. all-purpose flour
3 T. oil
2/3 c. water
4-oz. can sliced mushrooms

1-1/2 oz. pkg. onion soup mix
1 c. sour cream
cooked egg noodles, tossed
   with butter

Slice meat into thin strips diagonally across the grain; coat with
flour. Heat oil in a skillet and brown the beef; drain as needed.
Add water, mushrooms and their liquid to skillet; stir in soup
mix and heat just to boiling. Blend in sour cream. Serve over
buttered noodles.

No cooked, cubed ham on hand? Chop up some slices of cooked deli ham to use instead. Deli turkey, chicken and even roast beef can be used in place of cooked meats in recipes...what a timesaver!

Ham & Noodle Skillet

Makes 4 servings

2 c. cooked ham, cubed
1/4 c. onion, chopped
2 T. margarine
1/8 t. pepper
1/8 t. paprika
1 t. Worcestershire sauce

1 c. water
4-oz. can mushrooms, drained
 and 1/4 c. liquid reserved
4-oz. pkg. medium egg noodles,
 uncooked
1 c. sour cream

Sauté ham and onion in margarine; stir in pepper, paprika and Worcestershire sauce. Add water, reserved mushroom liquid and noodles; bring to a boil. Reduce heat; simmer, covered, for 15 minutes. Stir in mushrooms; heat for 5 minutes. Add sour cream; heat through without boiling.

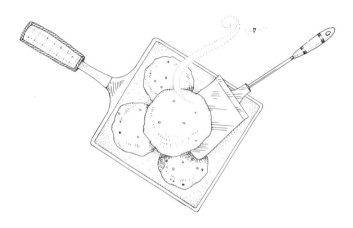

Crispy potato pancakes are a great way to use extra mashed potatoes. Stir an egg yolk and some minced onion into 2 cups potatoes. Form into patties and fry in butter until golden. Delicious with grilled sausage!

Simply Scrumptious Frittata

Makes 4 servings

1 T. oil
1/2 c. onion, chopped
1/2 c. green pepper, chopped
1 to 2 cloves garlic, minced
4 potatoes, peeled, cubed and
    cooked

3/4 c. cooked ham, cubed
8 eggs, beaten
salt and pepper to taste
3/4 c. shredded Cheddar
    cheese

Heat oil in a heavy oven-proof skillet over medium heat. Add onion and green pepper; cook and stir until tender. Add garlic; cook for an additional minute. Stir in potatoes and ham; cook until heated through. Reduce heat to medium-low; add eggs, salt and pepper. Cook until eggs are firm on the bottom, about 5 minutes. Top with cheese; place in oven at 350 degrees for 5 to 10 minutes, or until cheese melts. Cut into wedges.

A mini photo album is just right for keeping tried & true
recipes handy on the kitchen counter. Slide in a few
snapshots of happy family mealtimes too!

Chicken Pot Pie

Makes 6 servings

2 c. cooked chicken, chopped
15-oz. can mixed vegetables,
   drained
2 10-3/4 oz. cans cream of
   chicken soup

1 c. milk
10-oz. tube refrigerated
   biscuits

Combine first 4 ingredients together; place in an ungreased 3-quart
casserole dish. Bake at 400 degrees for 20 minutes. While baking,
slice biscuits into quarters; set aside. Remove dish from oven and
stir. Arrange biscuit pieces on top of hot chicken mixture; bake
until golden, 10 to 15 minutes.

Freezing cheese causes it to turn crumbly, and while that isn't good for a recipe using fresh cheese, it's ideal in baked casserole dishes! Just thaw cheese in the refrigerator and use within a few days.

Chili-Cheese Dog Casserole

Makes 8 servings

8-oz. tube refrigerated
   buttermilk biscuits
1/2 c. shredded Cheddar cheese

8 hot dogs
15-oz. can chili with beans

Flatten each biscuit into a 6-inch round; sprinkle with cheese. Place a hot dog near the edge of each round; roll up. Place seam-side down in a greased 13"x9" baking pan; bake at 375 degrees for 18 to 20 minutes. Top with chili; bake for an additional 5 minutes, until heated through.

Ah! There is nothing like staying at home for real comfort.

-Jane Austen

Penne Rustica

Makes 6 servings

1/4 c. olive oil
1-1/2 T. garlic, minced
1/2 c. onion, diced
3 c. broccoli flowerets, cut into
   bite-size pieces

1 c. chicken broth
16-oz. pkg. penne pasta,
   cooked
1/3 c. grated Parmesan cheese
salt and pepper to taste

Heat oil in a large skillet over medium heat; add garlic, onion and broccoli. Cook for 7 minutes, or until broccoli is tender. Add broth; simmer for 2 minutes. Place pasta in a large bowl; add broccoli mixture, cheese, salt and pepper. Toss to coat.

For a side dish that practically cooks itself, fill aluminum foil packets with sliced fresh veggies. Top with seasoning salt and 2 ice cubes, seal and bake at 450 degrees for 20 to 25 minutes. Delicious!

Saucy BBQ Chicken

Makes 3 to 4 servings

1-1/2 lbs. boneless, skinless
  chicken breasts
1/4 c. hot or mild salsa
1/4 c. catsup

1 T. onion soup mix
1 T. soy sauce
1/2 t. paprika
1/8 t. cayenne pepper

Arrange chicken in a microwave-safe dish and set aside. Combine remaining ingredients and spread over chicken to cover, using all of the mixture. Cover dish with a lid or with microwave-safe plastic wrap. Microwave on high setting for 5 minutes. Rearrange chicken pieces and cover again. Microwave on high an additional 3 to 6 minutes, until chicken juices run clear when pierced.

Set out all the fixin's for a spud-tacular potato bar for dinner tonight! Let the kids choose their favorite toppers...a fun way to personalize your potato.

Ham & Broccoli Baked Potatoes   *Makes 2 servings*

2 baking potatoes
1/2 c. cooked ham, chopped
1/2 c. broccoli, cooked and
    chopped

2 slices American cheese
Garnish: 2 t. green onion,
    chopped

Pierce potatoes with a fork; microwave for 6 to 8 minutes on high setting until tender. Cut lengthwise and crosswise; press open. Top each potato with 1/4 cup each of ham and broccoli. Top each with American cheese. Microwave an additional minute, or until cheese is melted; garnish with green onion.

If family members will be dining at different times, fix sandwiches ahead of time, wrap in aluminum foil and refrigerate. Pop them into a toaster oven or under a broiler to heat...fresh, tasty and ready when you are!

Grilled Salami Pizza Sandwiches   *Makes 4 servings*

2/3 c. pizza sauce
8 slices bread
4 slices deli salami

4 slices American cheese
garlic salt to taste
butter, softened

Spread pizza sauce on one side of 4 bread slices. Top each bread slice with one salami slice and one cheese slice; sprinkle with garlic salt. Top with remaining bread slices. Generously butter top and bottom of sandwiches. Heat a skillet over medium heat; add sandwiches and cook on both sides until bread is toasted and cheese is melted.

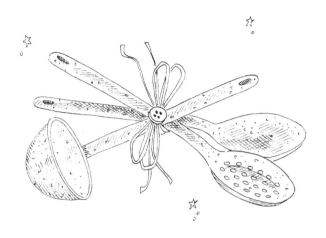

Make veggie or bean soups thick & creamy...simply purée a cup or so of the soup in a blender, then stir it back into the soup pot.

Italian Bean Soup

Makes 4 to 6 servings

1 lb. ground pork sausage
1 onion, chopped
1 clove garlic, minced
28-oz. can diced tomatoes
15-oz. can red kidney beans,
    drained and rinsed
14-1/2 oz. can beef broth

15-oz. can black beans, drained
    and rinsed
15-oz. can navy beans, drained
    and rinsed
2 T. grated Parmesan cheese
1 t. dried basil

Brown together sausage, onion and garlic in a stockpot over medium heat; drain. Add remaining ingredients; simmer until soup comes to a boil.

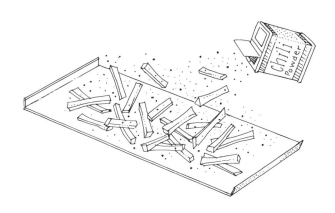

Spice up frozen French fries! Simply spritz with olive oil and sprinkle with chili powder before popping them in the oven.

Poor-Boy Sandwiches

Makes 2 to 3 servings

1 loaf French bread, sliced in
   half lengthwise
1/2 c. mayonnaise
1 c. shredded lettuce

1/2 lb. deli roast beef, thinly
   sliced
1/2 c. beef gravy, warmed
2 tomatoes, sliced

Warm bread in the oven. Remove from oven; spread bottom half with
mayonnaise. Layer with lettuce and roast beef; spoon gravy over
meat. Top with tomatoes; replace top half of bread. Cut into 2 or
3 slices; serve warm.

Cook up a big pot of vegetable soup. Save odds & ends of leftover veggies in a freezer bag. Thaw and place in a slow cooker along with 2 cans broth and 1/2 cup quick-cooking barley. Cook on low for 6 to 8 hours. So satisfying!

Busy-Day Vegetable Soup

Makes 6 servings

1 lb. ground beef, browned
2 28-oz. cans whole tomatoes, chopped
2 15-oz. cans mixed vegetables

3 bay leaves
1 onion, sliced

Combine ingredients in a large stockpot; stir to mix well. Bring to a boil; reduce heat and simmer for 20 to 25 minutes. Discard bay leaves before serving.

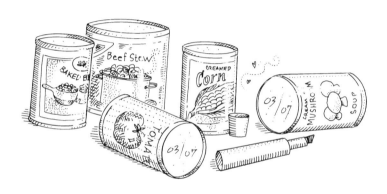

Keep a permanent marker handy in the kitchen to
write the purchase date on food cans and boxes...
you'll always know how fresh they are.

Fast Flavorful Tortilla Soup   *Makes 6 servings*

2 14-oz. cans chicken broth
10-oz. can chicken, drained
15-oz. can corn, drained
15-oz. can black beans, drained
   and rinsed

10-oz. can tomatoes with
   chiles, drained
13-1/2 oz. pkg. tortilla chips
Garnish: shredded Cheddar
   cheese

Combine all ingredients except chips and cheese in a large stockpot over medium heat; simmer until heated through, about 10 minutes. Serve over tortilla chips and garnish with cheese.

For a quick & tasty side, slice fresh tomatoes in half
and sprinkle with minced garlic, Italian seasoning and
grated Parmesan cheese. Broil until tomatoes
are tender, about 5 minutes...scrumptious!

Best-Ever Cornbread

Makes 4 servings

7-oz. pkg. cornbread mix
2 eggs
1/4 c. oil
1 c. sour cream

1 c. creamed corn
Optional: diced jalapeños
    to taste

Mix all ingredients together in a medium bowl. Pour into a lightly greased 8" round baking pan. Bake at 400 degrees for 35 minutes, or until golden. Serves 6 to 8.

Make clean-up a snap! Before dinner even starts, fill the sink with hot, soapy water. Put dishes right in when cooking's finished and, by the time dinner and dessert are eaten, they'll be a breeze to wash clean.

Sassy Salsa Rice

Makes 6 servings

3 T. butter
2 c. long-cooking rice,
    uncooked

14-oz. can chicken broth
24-oz. jar salsa

Melt butter in a large saucepan over medium heat; add rice and sauté
until golden. Add broth and salsa; bring to a boil. Reduce heat, cover
and simmer for 15 to 20 minutes, until rice is tender and liquid
is absorbed.

Take it easy and have a leftovers night once a week.
Set out leftovers so everyone can choose their favorite.
End with ice cream for dessert...what could be simpler?

Savory Succotash

Makes 4 to 6 servings

16-oz. pkg. frozen succotash
3/4 c. water
1/4 c. butter
1 onion, chopped

1 T. dried parsley
1 t. salt
1/2 t. pepper

Combine succotash and water in a saucepan; set aside. In a small skillet, melt butter and sauté onion over medium heat until transparent. Add onion to succotash along with remaining ingredients. Simmer over medium-low heat for 30 minutes, until tender.

Serving up baked potatoes with dinner? Rub the skins with butter and salt before baking...so delicious!

Upside-Down Baked Potatoes   *Makes 4 to 6 servings*

4 T. margarine, melted
2 T. grated Parmesan cheese

4 to 6 potatoes, cut in half
lengthwise

Coat bottom of a 13"x9" baking pan with margarine; sprinkle cheese on top. Place potatoes cut-side down in pan; bake at 400 degrees for 30 to 40 minutes, until tender.

Fresh veggies don't need to be fussy. A simple raw vegetable antipasto means forgetting about plates and forks with a tasty pick-up-and-munch snack.

Orange-Glazed Carrots

Makes 4 to 6 servings

16-oz. pkg. baby carrots
1/2 c. orange juice
5 T. brown sugar, packed

2 T. butter
1/8 t. salt

Place carrots in a medium saucepan. Cover with water and boil until tender; drain and return to saucepan. Add orange juice to saucepan; simmer over low heat until juice is nearly evaporated. Stir in remaining ingredients; heat until butter is melted and mixture is well blended.

Oh-so-easy iced tea...fill a 2-quart pitcher with water and drop
in 6 to 8 teabags. Refrigerate overnight. Discard teabags and
add ice cubes and sugar to taste. Cool and refreshing!

Lemon-Rice Pilaf

Makes 4 servings

2 T. butter
1/2 c. long-grain rice, uncooked
1/2 c. vermicelli, uncooked and
    broken into 1-inch pieces

1-3/4 c. chicken broth
1 T. lemon zest
1 t. dried parsley

Melt butter in a saucepan; add rice and vermicelli. Cook over medium heat until golden; add broth. Bring to a boil; reduce heat. Cover; simmer for 15 to 20 minutes. Stir in lemon zest and parsley.

Is dinner taking just a little longer than planned? Set out bowls
of unshelled walnuts or peanuts for a quick appetizer
that will keep tummies from rumbling.

Company Creamed Spinach

Makes 4 servings

10-oz. pkg. frozen chopped
    spinach
1 T. dried, minced onion

1-1/2 T. bacon bits
1/2 to 3/4 c. sour cream

Prepare spinach according to package directions; add onion and bacon bits to cooking water halfway through cooking time. Drain well; stir in sour cream to desired consistency.

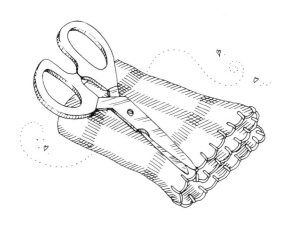

Keep a pair of kitchen scissors nearby for chopping
bacon, snipping green onions and opening packages...
you'll wonder what you ever did without them!

Creamy Macaroni & Cheese

Makes 4 servings

2 c. elbow macaroni, uncooked
1/4 lb. pasteurized process
   cheese spread, diced

salt and pepper to taste

Cook macaroni according to package directions; drain and return to pan. Stir in cheese until melted; add salt and pepper to taste.

Whip up a yummy salad in seconds! Purchase a bag of mixed
salad greens and toss in fruit, nuts and grated cheese.
Top off the salad with a drizzle of vinaigrette and toss.

Dijon Dressing

Makes about 1-1/4 cups

3/4 c. olive oil
3 T. sherry wine vinegar

3 T. lemon juice
1 T. Dijon mustard

Whisk together all ingredients and refrigerate. Shake well before serving.

Garlic Vinaigrette

Makes 1-3/4 cups

1-1/4 c. oil
1/2 c. wine vinegar
2 T. sugar

2 T. salt
1/4 t. pepper
6 cloves garlic, pressed

Blend together all ingredients and refrigerate. Stir or shake well before serving.

No muss, no fuss...toss salad fixings and dressing in a plastic zipping bag, spoon out the salad, then toss the bag!

Summertime Pasta Salad

Makes 4 servings

8-oz. pkg. tri-color rotini,
    cooked
1 cucumber, chopped
2 tomatoes, chopped

6 to 8 baby carrots, chopped
8-oz. bottle Italian salad
    dressing

Rinse pasta in cold water; drain and pour into a serving bowl.
Add remaining ingredients; toss to coat. Chill before serving.

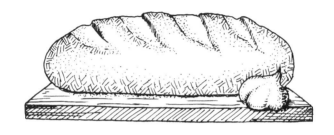

Homemade savory crackers are a special touch for soup.
Spread saltines with softened butter, then sprinkle with
garlic powder, thyme, paprika or another favorite seasoning.
Pop into a 350-degree oven just until golden, 3 to 6 minutes.

Onion French Bread

Makes 6 to 8 servings

1 loaf French bread, sliced in
   half lengthwise
1 c. mayonnaise

1/2 c. onion, chopped
1/2 c. grated Parmesan cheese
Garnish: paprika

Place bread on an ungreased baking sheet and set aside. Mix mayonnaise, onion and cheese; spread over cut side of bread. Sprinkle with paprika; broil for 3 to 5 minutes, or until golden. Slice and serve warm.

Bags of salad mix are real timesavers. Keep opened
bags of greens crispy by storing in airtight containers
or plastic zipping bags...just be sure to squeeze
out all the air before refrigerating.

Shoepeg Corn Salad

Makes 4 to 6 servings

2 11-oz. cans shoepeg corn,
   drained
2 stalks celery, diced
1/4 c. onion, chopped
1 green or red pepper, diced

8-oz. container sour cream
1/2 c. Caesar salad dressing
salt and pepper to taste
Garnish: paprika

Mix the first 6 ingredients together. Add salt and pepper to taste;
garnish with paprika. Chill.

Mmm…warm apple pie filling makes an oh-so-easy
dessert when spooned over vanilla ice cream!

Escalloped Apples

Makes 8 to 10 servings

10 c. tart apples, cored, peeled
   and sliced
1/3 c. sugar
2 T. cornstarch

1 t. cinnamon
1/4 t. nutmeg
2 T. chilled butter, sliced

Place apples in a 2-1/2 quart microwave-safe bowl; set aside.
Combine sugar, cornstarch, cinnamon and nutmeg; sprinkle over
apples. Toss gently to coat; dot with butter. Cover and microwave
on high until apples are tender, about 15 minutes, stirring every
5 minutes.

Serve up fruit salads in old-fashioned glass
compotes to let all the colors show through.

Frosty Fruit Salad

16-oz. pkg. frozen sliced
    strawberries, partially
    thawed
12-oz. can frozen orange juice
    concentrate, partially thawed

2 15-oz. cans fruit cocktail in
    syrup
20-oz. can crushed pineapple
    in juice
3 bananas, diced

Mix together all ingredients, including juices from fruit. Pour into a
13"x9" plastic freezer container; cover and freeze. To serve, let stand
at room temperature for 30 to 40 minutes. Scoop out portions with a
small ice cream scoop.

Forget about anything fussy...enjoy dessert outside
and let the crumbs fall where they may!

Lazy Day Bars

Makes 2 dozen

18-1/2 oz. pkg. German
   chocolate cake mix
2 eggs, beaten
1/4 c. water
1/4 c. brown sugar, packed

1/4 c. butter, softened
1/2 c. chopped nuts
12-oz. pkg. semi-sweet
   chocolate chips

Blend together dry cake mix, eggs, water, sugar and butter; spread in a greased 13"x9" baking pan. Sprinkle nuts and chips on top; bake at 350 degrees for 20 to 25 minutes. Cool for 10 minutes; cut into bars.

Line your brownie dish with aluminum foil...be sure to grease.
After brownies are baked and cooled, they lift right out.
And best of all, clean-up is a breeze!

Easy Lemon-Coconut Bars

Makes 1-1/2 dozen

18-1/4 oz. pkg. angel food
    cake mix
2/3 c. sweetened flaked coconut

14-1/2 oz. can lemon pie filling
Garnish: powdered sugar

In a medium bowl, stir dry cake mix, coconut and pie filling just until blended. Pour into an ungreased 15"x10" jelly-roll pan. Bake at 350 degrees for 20 to 30 minutes, or until center is firm. Sprinkle with powdered sugar; cut into squares.

Resist the urge to nibble on broken cookies...they make
tasty toppings sprinkled on a dish of ice cream!

Mother's No-Bake Cookies

Makes 6 to 7 dozen

4 c. sugar
1 c. margarine, softened
1 c. milk
6 T. baking cocoa
1 c. crunchy peanut butter

6 c. quick-cooking oats,
   uncooked
Optional: 1 c. walnuts,
1 c. sweetened flaked coconut

Combine sugar, margarine, milk and cocoa in a medium saucepan;
mix well. Bring to a boil over low heat; boil for one minute. Add
peanut butter, stirring until melted. Add oats and, if desired, nuts
or coconut. Mix well; drop by teaspoonfuls onto wax paper. Chill
until set.

Make your cookies all the same size! Use a mini ice cream
scoop to drop dough onto baking sheets, or
roll dough into a log, chill and slice.

No-Flour Peanut Butter Cookies

Makes 2 dozen

1 egg, beaten
1 c. sugar
1 t. baking soda

1 c. crunchy peanut butter
1 t. vanilla extract

Combine all ingredients; roll into 24 balls. Bake at 350 degrees on a lightly greased baking sheet for 10 to 12 minutes.

An easy way to core apples and peaches...slice fruit in half
and then use a melon baller to scoop out the core.

Caramel Apple Cake

Makes 4 to 6 servings

1-1/2 c. biscuit baking mix
2/3 c. sugar
1/2 c. milk
2 c. apples, cored, peeled and
    sliced

1 T. lemon juice
3/4 c. brown sugar, packed
1/4 t. cinnamon
1 c. boiling water
Garnish: whipped topping

Combine baking mix and sugar; stir in milk. Pour into a greased
9"x9" baking pan; top with apples. Sprinkle with lemon juice; set
aside. Mix brown sugar and cinnamon; sprinkle over apples. Pour
water over top; bake at 350 degrees for 50 minutes to one hour.
Serve with whipped topping.

Layer fresh berries with creamy vanilla pudding in
stemmed glasses for a festive dessert,
quick as a wink!

Peaches & Cream Dessert

Makes 8 to 10 servings

18-1/2 oz. pkg. yellow cake mix
1/2 c. butter, softened
14-1/2 oz. can peach pie filling
15-oz. can sliced peaches,
    drained

1/2 c. sugar
1 t. cinnamon
1 c. sour cream
1 egg, beaten

Combine dry cake mix with butter until crumbly; pat into an ungreased 13"x9" baking pan. Spread pie filling over top; lay peaches on pie filling. Set aside. Mix sugar and cinnamon; sprinkle over peaches. Blend sour cream and egg together; spread over sugar mixture. Bake at 350 degrees for 25 to 35 minutes, until edges are golden.

Day-old bread is fine for bread pudding and stuffing.
It keeps its texture better than very fresh bread...
it's thrifty too!

Golden Bread Pudding

Makes 4 to 6 servings

3 c. white bread, cubed
3 eggs, beaten
3 c. warm water
14-oz. can sweetened
   condensed milk

2 T. margarine, melted
1 T. vanilla extract
1/2 t. salt
Garnish: cinnamon-sugar

Place bread cubes in a buttered 9"x9" baking pan; set aside. In a large mixing bowl, combine all remaining ingredients except cinnamon-sugar; pour evenly over bread. Sprinkle with cinnamon-sugar. Bake at 350 degrees for 45 to 50 minutes. Serve warm.

Keep the cupboard stocked with a selection of colored jimmies,
chocolate bits and chopped peanuts
for quick ice cream toppings.

Fast Fruit & Cake Dessert

Makes 8 to 10 servings

1/4 c. oil
18-1/4 oz. pkg. yellow cake mix
2 eggs, beaten

1/2 c. water
21-oz. can cherry or blueberry
  pie filling

Pour oil into a 13"x9" baking pan; tilt to coat the bottom. Pour dry cake mix, eggs and water into pan. Stir with a fork until well blended, about 2 minutes. Spoon pie filling over batter and bake at 350 degrees for 35 to 45 minutes.

It's easy to make your own crumb crust. Mix 1-1/2 cups
fine crumbs, 1/4 cup sugar and 1/2 cup melted butter;
press into a pie plate. Chill for 20 minutes or bake at
350 degrees for 10 minutes. For the crumbs, use vanilla
wafers or graham crackers, of course...try fruit-flavored
cereal, gingersnaps or even pretzels too!

No-Bake Banana Cream Pie

Makes 8 servings

1 c. milk
3.4-oz. pkg. instant vanilla
   pudding mix
1/2 t. vanilla extract
12-oz. container frozen
   whipped topping, thawed
   and divided

9-inch vanilla wafer crumb
   crust
4 bananas, sliced

Combine milk and pudding mix in a large bowl; beat with an electric mixer on low speed for 2 minutes. Blend in vanilla. Fold in 3 cups whipped topping. Spread one cup of pudding mixture in pie crust; layer with sliced bananas. Repeat layering with another cup of pudding and remaining bananas, ending with remaining pudding. Top with remaining whipped topping. Chill before serving.

Use a pastry blender to slice or mash bananas
to desired consistency...so quick & easy!

Best-Ever Banana Bars

Makes 2 dozen

2 c. all-purpose flour
1-1/3 c. sugar
2 t. baking soda
1/2 t. salt

2 very ripe bananas, mashed
3/4 c. shortening, melted
4 eggs, beaten
2 t. vanilla extract

Combine flour, sugar, baking soda and salt in large mixing bowl; set aside. Mix bananas, shortening, eggs and vanilla in another mixing bowl; blend well. Add banana mixture to flour mixture; stir until just moistened. Pour into a greased 15"x10" jelly-roll pan; bake at 350 degrees for 20 minutes, or until center springs back when touched. Cut into bars.

Here's a handy shopping list! Stock up on these groceries when they're on sale...you'll be prepared for cheap & easy dinners and desserts anytime.

Pantry Foods

Canned Goods

☐ soup & chili beans
☐ diced tomatoes
☐ mixed vegetables
☐ cream soup
☐ chicken broth
☐ fruit pie filling

Boxed Goods

☐ pasta & macaroni
☐ rice & rice mix
☐ biscuit baking mix
☐ corn muffin mix
☐ cake mix
☐ crumb pie crusts
☐ instant pudding mix

Refrigerated & Frozen Foods

Butcher's Counter

- ☐ ground beef
- ☐ beef chuck roast
- ☐ boneless chicken breasts & thighs
- ☐ pork chops

Frozen Foods

- ☐ frozen vegetables
- ☐ frozen hashbrown potatoes
- ☐ frozen whipped topping

Refrigerator Case

- ☐ shredded cheese
- ☐ refrigerated biscuits, rolls, bread sticks
- ☐ refrigerated pie crusts

INDEX

INDEX

Our Story

Back in 1984, we were next-door neighbors raising our families in the little town of Delaware, Ohio. We were two moms with small children looking for a way to do what we loved and stay home with the kids too. We shared a love of home cooking and making memories with family & friends. After many a conversation over the backyard fence, **Gooseberry Patch** was born.

We put together the first catalog & cookbooks at our kitchen tables and packed boxes from the basement, enlisting the help of our loved ones wherever we could. From that little family, we've grown to include an amazing group of creative folks who love cooking, decorating and creating as much as we do.

Hard to believe it's been over 25 years since those kitchen-table days. Today, we're best known for our homestyle, family-friendly cookbooks. We love hand-picking the recipes and are tickled to share our inspiration, ideas and more with you! One thing's for sure, we couldn't have done it without our friends all across the country. Whether you've been along for the ride from the beginning or are just discovering us, welcome to our family!

Want to hear the latest from **Gooseberry Patch**?
www.gooseberrypatch.com

Join Our Circle of Friends

VIDEOS

Read Our Blog

Find us on Facebook

Follow us on twitter

Vickie & JoAnn

1•800•854•6673